MY
MISSING PET WORKBOOK

CAT EDITION

MY MISSING PET WORKBOOK
CAT EDITION

My Missing Pet Workbook: Cat Edition
ISBN: 978-1-7327803-7-8
Published in the United States of America

My Missing Pet Workbook: Cat Edition

TABLE OF CONTENTS

MY MISSING PET WORKBOOK
CAT EDITION

Dear Reader,

I am so sorry that you've lost a cherished member of your family. Please don't give up hope! Cats can survive the elements far better than we give them credit for.

We recently lost our beloved cat, Marie for two weeks. It was the longest two weeks of our lives. The weather was rainy, cold, and it even snowed one night. We searched for her daily, hung flyers, and canvassed the neighborhoods and businesses around our home. We were determined to find her.

I quickly became overwhelmed. Monitoring and responding to social media posts, advice, and sightings; actively canvassing the neighborhood while attempting to remember which homes we had already approached; physically searching nearby yards; calling and visiting animal shelters and veterinary clinics; and responding to possible sightings. After a few days we added humane traps and a dog tracking service to our efforts, which though helpful, added more items to my already complicated 'to do' list.

It wasn't long before I realized that I needed a notebook to record and keep track of our efforts. A single book to write the contact information for animal shelters, veterinary clinics, and rescues; to keep track of the online sites we had posted to; neighborhood sightings; camera, food, and trap placements; possible hiding spots the dog tracker team had identified, our 'lost pet' poster placements, and a record of the flyers we had delivered to local businesses and homes – to avoid duplication. This book is what I wished I had to compile our search data, so I hope it will help other pet owners experiencing similar loss.

Throughout this ordeal, we met many wonderful people. So many offered helpful advice, and suggestions to locate Marie. I have included this information and more in this book.

It is my hope that this notebook will make searching for your lost pet more efficient, effective, and organized.

Praying for a joyful reunion,

Janice, Wildrose Media

MY MISSING PET INFO

NAME:_____

DATE MISSING:_____

ESCAPED FROM:_____

MICROCHIP #:_____

WEARING COLLAR: Y N   SPAYED/NEUTERED: Y N

LAST SEEN:_____

BREED: _____

COLORING:_____

AGE:_____

WEIGHT:_____

INDOOR ONLY CAT: Y N   INDOOR/OUTDOOR CAT: Y N

MARKINGS:_____

_____

_____

_____

SPECIAL NEEDS:_____

_____

_____

CHARACTERISTICS: (shy/skittish/friendly, etc.)

_____

_____

MY VETERINARY CLINIC INFO:_____

_____

_____

MISSING CAT BEHAVIOR

Vocalization:
Will not usually meow if hiding outside- meowing will give away their hiding spot to other animals. This is especially true if your pet is in 'survival mode'. Their instincts take over. He or she may not recognize you as their loving owner.

Inclement Weather:
Cats are not likely to venture from their hiding spot during bad weather, such as rain. Once the weather clears, even if during the day, shake their food and call to them as you would in the evening.

DO NOT place your cat's litter box outside!
This may attract feral or more aggressive cats to your home, which if your cat is hiding nearby will force your pet to remain in hiding or to move further away from home.

Indoor Only Cats
Will often stay close to home, usually only a few (3-4) houses away.

Outdoor access cats (Indoor/Outdoor cats):
Cats who routinely have access to the outdoors usually will not go missing without cause. Cats are territorial creatures and it could be that your cat was chased off by another cat and is too frightened to return to its home turf.
Outdoor access cats often do not wander far, usually no further than 17 houses away. This distance may increase depending on the cat's ability to safely hide and be accepted onto another cat's territory.
Many indoor/outdoor cats return on their own after 10-12 days.

Searching Tips:
A PHYSICAL SEARCH FOR YOUR CAT IS MOST IMPORTANT!

You should obtain permission prior to searching someone's private property.
Ask your neighbors if you can search their yard yourself. (Most neighbors will not conduct as extensive search as you will, so don't rely on their word- that 'they looked').
Wear old clothes and don't be afraid to get dirty. Carry a flashlight and wear gloves.
- Crawl on your belly to look under tarps, overturned wheelbarrows, and garden items.
- Look under bushes, sheds, decks, garages, and houses. These are all areas where cats like to hide.
- Look inside sheds, garages, and vehicles- your pet may be trapped inside.

Cats climb, so don't forget to look up!
- in trees, on woodpiles, on roofs, and carports- including exposed rafters.

Cats will usually be most active from dusk until dawn, so searching during evening and early morning hours may be most productive.

TO DO LIST

Try to do the things on this list as soon as possible!

- ☐ Alert your immediate neighbors to keep an eye out for your pet.
  Most cats do not stray too far from home.
- ☐ Gather your pet's information- microchip #, weight, breed, markings, etc.
  (write it in the first page of this journal for easy reference)
- ☐ Find a digital, color photo which clearly shows your pet's face and markings.
  You will use this photo for your flyers and online/social media posts.
- ☐ Find or print a few color photos of your pet, you will use these on posters.
- ☐ Call local Veterinary Clinics to alert them your pet is missing.
- ☐ Create online posts with missing pet information (see "online posts" page).
- ☐ Create flyers to post and distribute locally (see "creating a flyer" page).
- ☐ Carefully place your pets bedding or blanket in a clean plastic bag. Do not wash!
  (avoid touching it too much- can be used for scenting a tracker dog if needed).
- ☐ Place an article of unwashed clothing, bedding (pillowcase), or towel at your front
  and back door. The scent may assist a disoriented cat find its way home.
- ☐ Make a temporary shelter by turning a plastic bin on its side.
  Place blankets or towels inside the bin. A large Styrofoam cooler with a
  hole cut in the side may also be used. Place a shelter in the front and back
  of your home, near the scent article.
- ☐ Your pet will be most active from dusk to dawn. Try shaking a bag of treats
  and calling your pet's name softly while searching with a flashlight.
- ☐ Go out after dark with a flashlight and search under porches, sheds, etc.
  The light will catch the reflection of your cat's eyes.
  Be sure to get permission before entering someone's yard or property.
- ☐ Go door to door in your community, distributing flyers.
  Include "snack bags" with several flyers - small amounts of dry cat food for
  neighbors to put outside. This food will help keep your cat in the area.
  *Note- not everyone likes cats, and some will object to placing food outside
  their door. They may believe it will invite strays or rodents to their porch.
- ☐ Obtain a humane trap or contact a rescue group which offers trapping services.
- ☐ Create a "chum trail". Add a can of cat food to a gallon jug and fill jug with warm
  water. Shake well. Sprinkle this mixture on the ground in a trail, leading to your
  door or the cat trap, if set.
- ☐ Create a "scent trail". Use unwashed laundry to cut strips of fabric.
  These strips should measure about 1" x 3" in size. Place these on the ground
  in a trail, leading to where you wish your animal to walk- front/back door
  or trap.
- ☐ File a missing pet report with your local animal shelter(s).
  Find out when visiting and adoption hours are.
  Plan on visiting these shelters every 2-3 days, "just in case".

DO NOT PLACE YOUR CAT'S LITTER PAN OUTSIDE!

CREATING FLYERS AND SIGNS

The best way to find your pet is to make others aware he or she is missing!
You will want to create signs and print flyers to distribute door to door among
neighbors, hang on telephone poles, and place inside/outside nearby businesses.
Flyers will need to be refreshed after about 1-2 weeks, so people will be aware
your pet is still missing (and the poster/flyer is still active rather than forgotten).
I have provided a sample flyer and sign on the next pages to use as a template.

Items to include in your flyer:
- Date missing
- If refreshing a flyer, include new flyer date and the words "still missing".
- Missing from location, including zip code and street names (include cross
  street), and community name. If desired, you can include a landmark or building
  to identify an area, such as "across from Smith's Jewelry Store".
- Last location your pet was spotted, if any.
- If micro chipped, spayed/neutered, wearing collar (include color of the collar).
- Specific identifying markings (green eyes, cropped tail, etc.).
- Specific instructions, such as "do not chase".
- Specific instructions if you include a 'snack pack' with your flyer., such as where
  and when to put the food out. (i.e. on back porch at night only).
- To check in garages, sheds, and under porches. These are favorite places for
  animals to hide.
- Your cell phone number.
- Reward (you do not need to include amount, and it need not be monetary).
- _____

GATHER SUPPLIES

- ☐ color photos of your pet (one for each poster board sign)
- ☐ Clear plastic page protectors
- ☐ tape (waterproof is best)
- ☐ scissors
- ☐ a stapler and staples
- ☐ white copy paper for flyers
- ☐ ink for printer if printing at home
- ☐ neon yellow or orange poster board
- ☐ cardboard or stiff backer board for mounting poster board, if needed
- ☐ markers
- ☐ wooden stakes or wire frames for securing large signs
- ☐ _____
- ☐ _____

SAMPLE SIGN FOR BUSINESSES, TELEPHONE POLES

* Note - the photo should be color, if possible

Still missing 12-5-19 Please help!

Missing Cat

"MARIE" Lost 11-27-19

CROSS STREETS, ZIPCODE,COMMUNITY

10 lbs, green eyes, has microchip, no collar

CALL or TEXT XXX-XXX-XXXX anytime

Please do not chase!

REWARD

Please look in garages, sheds and under porches
She may be trapped.
If you can let her inside without chasing her, please try. It's cold!

SAMPLE FLYER FOR NEIGHBORS

**note- you can add color to highlight the bold text and phone numbers
- the photo should be color, if possible

Please Help! REWARD Offered! Updated 12-6-19

Our cat, MARIE has been missing since before Thanksgiving (11-27-19).
She is 4 years old, has brown, orange, and black stripes.
White chest and paws. White stripe between her eyes. Green eyes.
No collar. Weighs 10 lbs, so a medium sized cat.
She is microchipped, which means any vet can scan her and contact us.
11-28-19 spotted near XXX Lane and XXX Rd

Please, we are asking your help:
We have provided some of her food.
Would you please place it in a bowl on your **back porch**, with a bowl of water?
If not, would please you call us to pick up the food?
(we know not everyone likes cats, and don't want stray animals around).
If you see the food has been eaten, please call us.
If you see her, please watch where she goes and call us immediately.

ALSO!! Please check in and under your porch, decks, sheds, and garage.
We have been advised to reach as many homes nearby as we can.
If you see her nearby, please call us asap.
She will likely be active from dark to early morning (5pm to 6am).
Do not try to chase her, for two reasons:
• She is very skittish and will run, possibly pushing her further away.
• She may be in 'survival mode' and not be friendly. She's cute but may bite or scratch- even us her owners as she is scared.

IF YOU HAVE HER IN YOUR HOME- THANK YOU!!
But- please know Marie is deeply loved and missed by her family.
Please return her to us, we will be forever grateful.
WE ARE OFFERING A REWARD
XXX-XXX-XXXX call or text 24/7

PLACES to POST FLYERS and/or SIGNS:

Once your flyers are complete, slip them inside a plastic sleeve.
Insert the paper so that the opening is at the bottom. This will prevent the paper from getting wet in case of rain. Place a small piece of tape to seal the bottom, to prevent the flyer paper from falling out.

- Veterinary clinics
- Pet stores
- Near schools
- Churches
- Libraries
- Grocery stores
- Pharmacies
- Banks
- Coffee shops
- Restaurants
- Gas stations
- In your vehicle window
- On telephone poles
- _____
- _____
- _____

Use the flyer log and neighborhood grid provided in this notebook to keep track where the flyers are distributed.

Remember to remove these flyers once your pet is found

POSTING ONLINE

You need to have as many people looking for your pet as possible.

Online missing pet groups and neighborhood sites are great places to post missing pets.

Online sites to consider posting your lost pet include:

- Facebook – your personal page

* do not be afraid to ask your FB friends to share your post!

- Facebook Pet Groups (see suggestions below)
- Next Door
- Neighborhood Sites
- Community Pages
- Ring App
- Instagram
- Craigslist *do not accept a request for a code from someone claiming to have your pet- it is a scam! No code is needed to contact you- they already have – to ask for a code!

To find lost and found pet groups on Facebook, type in keywords such as:

- ❏ Lost and found pets in ------- (your county name)
- ❏ Lost and found pets in ------- (your city name)
- ❏ Missing pets in -------- (city)
- ❏ Missing pets in -------- (county)
- ❏ -------- county missing pets
- ❏ Cat rescue groups
- ❏ Dog rescue groups
- ❏ Pets - lost and found in --------
- ❏ Pet rescue of -------

** write each of these groups on your online posting record, to keep track of where and when you are posting. This will make it easier to notify these sites, (and thus their members) when your animal is found**

TRAPS AND TRACKERS...

If your cat has not returned home in a day or two, you may want to think about other options to locate him or her.

Humane Traps

Unlike dogs, most cats do not respond to their names, even under normal circumstances. A cat which is outdoors may be frightened and unwilling to come out from hiding, even when an owner is nearby. Your pet may be in 'survival mode' and not recognize you. For this reason, using a humane trap may be the best way to recover your cat.

Traps can be purchased at local hardware stores or online.

Traps can be rented from some animal shelters or rescue groups.

* get a size 30-inch trap for 10 lb. cat (aka 'raccoon size').
* get a size 36-inch trap for a larger cat.

Put the food directly on the trap's surface behind the trigger mechanism- do not use a plate or tray. Smart cats will stand back and scoop the food off the plate, thus avoiding the trigger mechanism!

Cover the front metal part of the trap with dirt, cardboard or a magnetic strip so your cat won't feel the transition from ground to trap.

Place small dollops of food in 1-2 locations leading towards the trap. These little 'bite-sized' snacks will (should!) entice the cat into the trap for the 'big food prize'.

Try to hide (disguise) the trap under a bush or between a house and garage BUT be sure the trap door can close completely to secure your animal.

In inclement weather, check the trap frequently- every 2 hours or more often if very cold. Trapped animals can freeze and get frostbite.

In rainy/wet weather, cover the trap with a waterproof material such as plastic bag, then cover with the scent article to help protect the cat.

It is advised to cover the trap with a 'scent article' such as a towel or blanket to attract your pet.

Place smelly food inside the trap- tuna, heated wet cat food, or sardines are good choices.

If you catch an animal that is not yours (it happens!), release it if wild (raccoon, etc.). If another cat, call animal control to pick it up, or take it to the nearest shelter. Please protect the trapped animal from the elements- *bring the trap inside* where it is warm (or cool, if summer), offer it water. If unsure about letting a stray animal into your home, you can *leave it inside the trap* for a *short while* until help arrives- but only if it looks 'healthy'.

Tracker Dogs

Specially trained dogs can conduct searches for missing animals.

These services are usually not free, and can be quite expensive but they offer hope, and for some, peace of mind. Just knowing your cat is nearby can be comforting- though frustrating! (why don't they just come inside?!.)

These tracking dogs work off a scent article, such as your cat's pillow or blanket. Therefore, as mentioned earlier, it is important to place the cat's pillow or blanket in a plastic bag and not wash the item until after your pet has returned home.

To locate a tracking team in your area, search online or ask for references from veterinary clinics or rescues.

A WORD ABOUT MICROCHIPS

A microchip is not a tracking device!
Its effectiveness is dependent on your animal being brought to a facility with a microchip scanner or has access to one themselves (as some pet rescues do).
For an actual tracking device, GPS units are available (most secure to a collar).
Microchips, once placed must be registered and activated.
This requires paying a fee.
Microchips can be scanned and traced back to the company which owns it, even if it has not been activated.
This company is then able to trace the ID number back to the owner *provided* the company has a current phone number on file.
All stray pets entering a facility such as a clinic or shelter *should* be scanned for a microchip.
Some clinics also re-scan for a microchip prior to the animal leaving the facility, such as for adoption.
Microchips have been known to occasionally migrate or move around inside the animal's body. This means that there is a possibility (though rare) that a microchip may not be picked up by a scanner.

A thought...
If someone thought your animal was a stray, they may have taken them into their home, believing they were helping an unwanted animal.
Not everyone will take a stray to animal control or the veterinary clinic immediately.
Some people keep or even rehome these animals themselves, though this is not recommended, and is against animal control policy in most states.
Call your local vet and ask what their protocol is for scanning pets on visits.
Your pet may not be discovered until it is brought in for a routine exam by its new 'owners'.

Deceased Animals
According to the shelters I spoke with, deceased animals which are brought in are also scanned, so the owner can be contacted. This may vary by state and county.
Our sincerest condolences if this is your pet's fate. May they rest in peace.
You did everything you could to locate them. They knew you loved them. Hugs.

SHELTERS, VETS, AND RESCUES

(Include business name & address, initial contact date, visit dates, and notify when found)

Name, Address, and Contact Person	Date	Call or Visit				Found

SHELTERS, VETS, AND RESCUES

(Include business name & address, initial contact date, visit dates, and notify when found)

Name, Address, and Contact Person	Date	Call or Visit				Found

SHELTERS, VETS, AND RESCUES

(Include business name & address, initial contact date, visit dates, and notify when found)

Name, Address, and Contact Person	Date	Call or Visit				Found

ONLINE POSTING RECORD

(Include page name, date posted, shares, and reposts. Don't forget to notify when found!)

Social Media Type and Page Name	Post	Re-Post			Found

ONLINE POSTING RECORD

(Include page name, date posted, shares, and reposts. Don't forget to notify when found!)

Social Media Type and Page Name	Post	Re-Post	Found

ONLINE POSTING RECORD

(Include page name, date posted, shares, and reposts. Don't forget to notify when found!)

Social Media Type and Page Name	Post	Re-Post	Found

ONLINE POSTING RECORD

(Include page name, date posted, shares, and reposts. Don't forget to notify when found!)

Social Media Type and Page Name	Post	Re-Post	Found

FLYER PLACEMENT RECORD

(include business name, whether allowed flyer, and dates flyer posted and removed)

Business and Contact Info.	Y/N	Up	Down

FLYER PLACEMENT RECORD

(include business name, whether allowed flyer, and dates flyer posted and removed)

Business and Contact Info.	Y/N	Up	Down

FLYER PLACEMENT RECORD

(include business name, whether allowed flyer, and dates flyer posted and removed)

Business and Contact Info.	Y/N	Up	Down

FLYER PLACEMENT RECORD

(include business name, whether allowed flyer, and dates flyer posted and removed)

Business and Contact Info.	Y/N	Up	Down

FLYER PLACEMENT RECORD

(include business name, whether allowed flyer, and dates flyer posted and removed)

Business and Contact Info.	Y/N	Up	Down

FLYER PLACEMENT RECORD

(include business name, whether allowed flyer, and dates flyer posted and removed)

Business and Contact Info.	Y/N	Up	Down

FLYER PLACEMENT RECORD

(include business name, whether allowed flyer, and dates flyer posted and removed)

Business and Contact Info.	Y/N	Up	Down

NEIGHBORHOOD CANVASSING GRID

DATE: _____

- Each square represents a house, add house numbers, cross streets
- Note the action taken at each house as follows:

Flyer: **FL**   Camera: **C**   Possible Sighting (add date): **P**
Food: **FD**   Scent article: **SA**   Shelter: **SH**

Street Name: Street Name: Street Name:

NEIGHBORHOOD CANVASSING GRID

DATE: _____

- Each square represents a house, add house numbers & cross streets
- Note the action taken at each house as follows:

Flyer: **FL**   Camera: **C**   Possible Sighting (add date): **P**

Food: **FD**   Scent article: **SA**   Shelter: **SH**

Street Name: Street Name: Street Name:

NEIGHBORHOOD CANVASSING GRID

DATE: _____

- Each square represents a house, add house numbers & cross streets
- Note the action taken at each house as follows:

Flyer: **FL**   Camera: **C**   Possible Sighting (add date): **P**
Food: **FD**   Scent article: **SA**   Shelter: **SH**

Street Name: _____

Street Name: _____

Street Name: _____

NEIGHBORHOOD CANVASSING GRID

DATE: _____

- Each square represents a house, add house numbers & cross streets
- Note the action taken at each house as follows:

Flyer: **FL**   Camera: **C**   Possible Sighting (add date): **P**

Food: **FD**   Scent article: **SA**   Shelter: **SH**

Street Name:

Street Name:

Street Name:

NEIGHBORHOOD CANVASSING GRID

DATE: _____

- Each square represents a house, add house numbers & cross streets
- Note the action taken at each house as follows:

Flyer: **FL**   Camera: **C**   Possible Sighting (add date): **P**

Food: **FD**   Scent article: **SA**   Shelter: **SH**

Street Name:

Street Name:

Street Name:

NEIGHBORHOOD CANVASSING GRID

DATE: _____

- Each square represents a house, add house numbers & cross streets
- Note the action taken at each house as follows:

Flyer: **FL** Camera: **C** Possible Sighting (add date): **P**
Food: **FD** Scent article: **SA** Shelter: **SH**

Street Name:

Street Name:

Street Name:

NEIGHBORHOOD CANVASSING GRID

DATE: _____

- Each square represents a house, add house numbers & cross streets
- Note the action taken at each house as follows:

Flyer: **FL**　　　　Camera: **C**　　　　Possible Sighting (add date): **P**

Food: **FD**　　　　Scent article: **SA**　　Shelter: **SH**

Street Name:　　　　Street Name:　　　　Street Name:

NEIGHBORHOOD CANVASSING GRID

DATE: _____

- Each square represents a house, add house numbers & cross streets
- Note the action taken at each house as follows:

Flyer: **FL**   Camera: **C**   Possible Sighting (add date): **P**
Food: **FD**   Scent article: **SA**   Shelter: **SH**

Street Name:

Street Name:

Street Name:

NEIGHBORHOOD CANVASSING GRID

DATE: _____

- Each square represents a house, add house numbers & cross streets
- Note the action taken at each house as follows:

Flyer: **FL**   Camera: **C**   Possible Sighting (add date): **P**

Food: **FD**   Scent article: **SA**   Shelter: **SH**

Street Name:

Street Name:

Street Name:

MONTH:

Sunday	Monday	Tuesday	Wednesday	Thursday	Friday	Saturday

MONTH:

Sunday	Monday	Tuesday	Wednesday	Thursday	Friday	Saturday

MONTH:

Sunday	Monday	Tuesday	Wednesday	Thursday	Friday	Saturday

MONTH:

Sunday	Monday	Tuesday	Wednesday	Thursday	Friday	Saturday

NOTES

NOTES

NOTES

NOTES

NOTES

WHAT TO DO WHEN YOUR PET IS FOUND

Congratulations!
Give them a big hug and a kiss!
What a relief- take a deep breath and let those tears flow...

If her or she appears to be in distress, do not hesitate to take them to the nearest pet care center for care.
There are 24-hour emergency veterinary clinics in all states.

If he or she does not appear to be in distress, call your vet as soon as possible to let them know your cat is home. You can discuss with the clinic the need to book an appointment and other concerns.

- Your pet's voice may be hoarse, can be from lack of water or loud and persistent vocalizing (meowing). This should improve in a couple of days.
- Closely examine them for cuts, scratches, puncture wounds, frostbite, ticks, thorns and other hazards.
- Look at their paws for cracks, glass or other foreign objects.
- Offer small amounts of food (about 1 Tablespoonful for cats) every 30 minutes or so. This will help prevent vomiting in an animal which hasn't eaten in awhile.
- Offer fresh water as soon as possible.
- Provide a warm, dry bed for them to sleep on, they may be exhausted.
- Notify the missing pet Facebook groups and online neighborhood pages such as *Nextdoor* that your pet is home safe.
- Call or visit the area businesses where you posted your flyers, so you (or they) can take them down.
- Remove your posters from the neighborhood telephone poles.
- Call the animal shelters and veterinary clinics to notify them your pet is home.
- Look into taking measures to prevent this from happening again. GPS pet trackers or other locator devices may be useful.

Have a success story to share?

We'd love to hear about your pet's successful return, and how this journal helped with the search. Please email us at **wildrosemedia18@gmail.com**

Interested in ordering copies of this this book in bulk?
Would you like copies personalized with your Rescue's name?

If you are an animal shelter employee, volunteer, or rescue group and are interested in purchasing these books in bulk for a discount, please contact Wildrose Media at **wildrosemedia18@gmail.com**

www.wildrose-media.com

ADDITIONAL BOOKS BY WILDROSE MEDIA

- Our Family Journal, an annual list of family favorites
- 100 Fun Questions to Ask Myself (a 3-year journal)- Volumes 1-3
- All About Me, An Art Journal for Kids – four cover styles to choose from
- Christmas & Holiday Card Checklist Books
- Holiday Preparation Book
- Bridal Shower Guestbook
- Baby Shower Guestbook
- Headache Diary
- Social Media Workbook
- Blog Post Planner
- 2020 Weekly and Monthly Planner
- Fitness and Weight Loss Tracker
- Sermon Notebooks
- Prayer Workbook for Kids
- Mini (5" x 6") Blank Notebooks and Sketchbooks
- Composition Notebooks & Blank Sketchbooks
- Coloring Books for Christmas and Easter
- Love Came Down, a Christmas Devotional

Join our mailing list for updates and new releases:
www.wildrose-media.com
Share your comments and reviews:
wildrosemedia18@gmail.com

www.ingramcontent.com/pod-product-compliance
Lightning Source LLC
Chambersburg PA
CBHW080628030426
42336CB00018B/3116